NO LONGER NAMELESS

A journey to discovering your true identity

THE ESV GLOBAL STUDY BIBLE®, ESV® BIBLE
COPYRIGHT © 2012 BY CROSSWAY.
ALL RIGHTS RESERVED.
THE HOLY BIBLE, ENGLISH STANDARD VERSION® (ESV®)
© 2001 BY CROSSWAY,
A PUBLISHING MINISTRY OF GOOD NEWS PUBLISHERS.
ALL RIGHTS RESERVED.

THE MESSAGE: THE BIBLE IN CONTEMPORARY LANGUAGE
COPYRIGHT © 2002 BY EUGENE H. PETERSON. ALL RIGHTS RESERVED.
THE MESSAGE NUMBERED EDITION COPYRIGHT © 2005
VERSION 2.0

DEDICATED TO MY MAMA, REBECCA BALLARD

THIS BOOK IS AN ANSWER TO YOUR PRAYERS AND JUST THE BEGINNING OF THINGS YOU SPOKE OVER ME. I THANK GOD FOR BLESSING ME WITH SUCH A WONDERFUL EXAMPLE OF A PROVERBS 31 WOMAN. THANK YOU FOR YOUR SACRIFICES, YOUR UNCONDITIONAL LOVE AND SUPPORT THROUGHOUT MY LIFE. THE MESSAGE OF THIS BOOK IS A CONTINUATION OF THE WORK YOU DID AND THE COUNTLESS LIVES YOU TOUCHED WHILE ON EARTH FOR THE KINGDOM OF GOD. MAY HE RECIEVE ALL THE GLORY.

I'LL SEE YOU IN THE AIR

TABLE OF CONTENTS
///////////

Chapter 1- Origins

Chapter 2 - Tangled

Chapter 3- Loved

Chapter 4- Fearless

Chapter 5- Beyond Compare

Chapter 6- That's Not My Name

Chapter 7- Follow Me

Introduction

My prayer as you read and work through this book is that you would establish where you are now and how you view your identity in life, but also that you would walk away from this book being forever changed. Having boldness, confidence, strength , and wisdom that you never had before, not from me, but from the Holy Spirit -from your Father God.

One of the things I love most about having a relationship with Jesus Christ is that
He meets you where you are, He doesn't tell you to clean up your act first, He meets you in your darkest places, but He doesn't leave you there. If you surrender to Him, He will always change you, challenge you, and transform you into the person that He created you to be, the person that He sees in the future, the person you long to be. You will go from being lost, confused,feeling like no matter what you do it's never good enough-into a person who knows their purpose, who knows their calling, and who walks confidently in it, without apology, and without doubt. A person who doesn't shrink back for fear of offending others, or feeling inadequate to fulfill the calling that God has placed on your life. I pray that as you work through this book that He would begin to renew your mind to break down strongholds and uproot all the lies that you have believed about yourself and about who you are, and would replace them with deep roots of love, purpose,peace, and authority in Him alone.
This journey may be painful at times as you look back on your life and discover where these seeds were first planted that took root in your mind and heart, recognizing who told you who you were or weren't, but there is purpose in the pain. Keep going, don't stop short of the promise. A tree doesn't grow in one day, in fact a lot of the growth has to happen under the surface first before you can sprout, but that is the most important work that must be done, that is the foundation of who you are. That is where deep and strong roots can grow so that next time a storm comes, you will not be moved, you will not be blown down, you will stand strong and firm in who you are and whose you are. Remember during this process it may feel like you've been buried, but you've just been planted..and when God plants a seed in good soil, its only a matter of time before the ground breaks and you sprout!

CHAPTER 1
Origins

Chapter 1
Origins

As we begin I would like to reiterate that this book, though challenging will begin to establish in you the foundation on which God's plans for your life can finally start to take shape. This is not a self-help book to help you gain more confidence, likes/ comments or validation from others. In fact my prayer is that it will do the exact opposite, that in the absence of those things you will still stand firm in what you believe, and who you are. Because the truth of the matter is that if we rise and fall with the praise or insults of others,we are no different than the rest of the world. We are called to be set apart. God wants us to be..

Like a tree planted by streams of water that yields its fruit in its season, and its leaf does not wither. In all that he does, he prospers. Psalm 1:3

This is an interactive book, so what you put into it, you will get out of it. Let's get started!

I'd like you to take some time on this page and reflect on who you think you are. How would you describe yourself? There is no right or wrong answer here, it is an honest inventory of your life, no judgments allowed, just observations..positive AND negative.

Ok, now take a good look at that list.. by the end of this book I pray that something inside you shifts and changes your perspective of yourself. I pray instead of seeing all the "flaws" you see space for improvement and growth.. or maybe even see that it's already begun.

I mentioned earlier about seeds being planted and finding the root of a belief or mindset, and I want to take you back to a story in the Bible that is a perfect example of how a small seed(thought) that is put into us and takes root, can drastically change our lives and the way we live everyday.

Let's begin with a little backstory so we can have proper context. In **Genesis 1:26-31**, God has created the heavens and the earth, animals, plants etc, and on the 6th day He created mankind. In this picture we see God's character that He is a God of order. He did not create man until last because He made everything else for us to enjoy and to sustain us first..He didn't create fish until after creating the oceans that would hold them, He made the earth and sun before vegetation..He made a space for us first before creating man. What a good Father! That detail in and of itself shows His love for us. So the next time you're tempted to think you don't fit in anywhere or you take up too much space in this world, come back to this story and remember He created the space before creating you!

Now let's keep digging..after creating Adam and Eve He calls them "very good" Mankind is the only thing in creation that is created in the image and likeness of God. This is called "Imago Dei" which means "Image of God" but what does it mean to be made in His image? I believe part of this means that as God is 3 in 1 (Father, Son, Holy Spirit) we are also 3 in 1 a.physical body, b.soul-(our mind, will and emotions)- and c. spirit-(the part of us that connects us to God) and we are to bear His image in the world..in other words we represent Him! This is the basic foundation of our identity.

SPIRIT
The part of us that is eternal, and connects us to God

SOUL
Mind, Will and Emotions

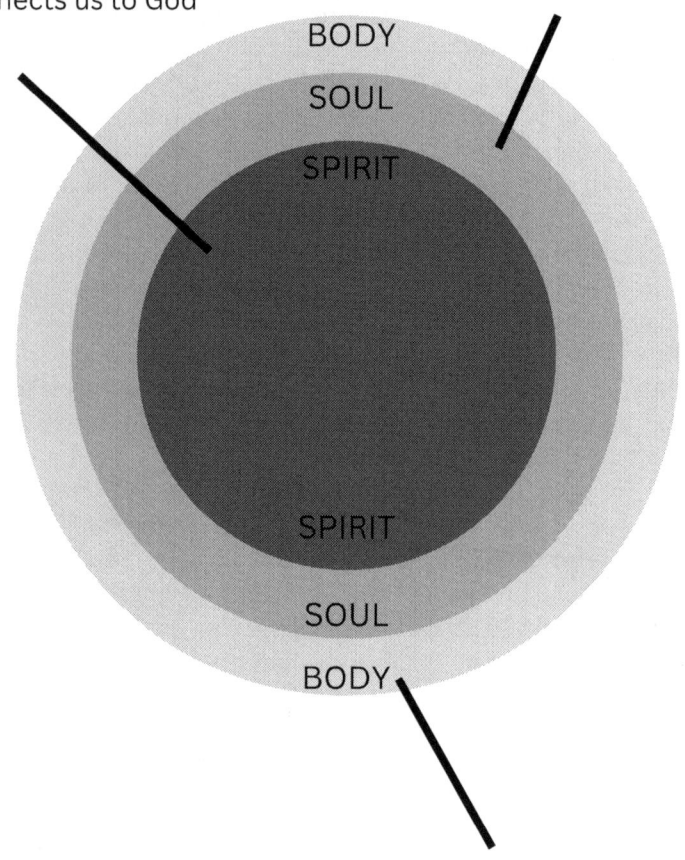

BODY
SOUL
SPIRIT

SPIRIT
SOUL
BODY

BODY
Our physical flesh that God created from the dust of the Earth

After creating them he calls them "very good" . How often do you look at yourself and think that you are "very good"? Have you ever had that thought about yourself? As a creative person myself, when I create something and I'm proud of it, I want someone to appreciate the work I put into it. If we really sit back and think there's a lot of things that God thoughtfully and intentionally made in our world and even in our own bodies that we take for granted every day. The very breath you are breathing, the blood pumping through your veins, the synapses in your brain all working in their original design just as he intended without you having to try, it's pretty amazing!

Let's continue, after creating Adam and Eve , they are happily walking in the garden just living it up. Can you imagine living in the most perfect garden walking with God and the one that you love that was created just for you without a care in the world? All of your needs provided everything that looks beautiful, perfectly content naked and all. In Genesis chapter 3 all that changes. You see, God had created everything for them to enjoy, but they had one rule: the tree in the midst of the garden was off limits; they had so much freedom and so many options and were perfectly content until now.. Eve is being tempted by the serpent (satan) to eat the fruit that God specifically told them not to eat. Satan didn't outright oppose what God told them, he first caused her to question what God actually said.. and herein lies the seed of doubt.

Although small, seeds contain information that holds the potential for big things. Deeply woven into this seed was another question that made her wonder what good things God might actually be withholding from them.. afterall satan told her that the reason God forbid this fruit was so that they wouldn't be like Him. Now Eve didn't have the Bible to look at like we do, but she had God himself and a relationship with him! In **Psalm 84:11** God's word says **No good thing does he withhold from those who walk uprightly.**

If Adam and Eve had trusted God's goodness over the enemy's lies perhaps when God had seen that they were faithful and had the character to handle this knowledge he might have given it to them anyway. The same goes for us ,sometimes when God isn't answering our prayers when or how we want him to, it's because he knows it would destroy us in this season. It doesn't mean that we will never have it or that he is keeping blessings from you like Satan wants us to believe. But a blessing in the wrong season can become a curse. If we truly trust God's goodness we must also trust his timing. We also see in scripture that God is the Spirit of wisdom and understanding (**Isaiah 11:2**) So this tells us that what they wanted was really more of Him! That sneaky snake caused them to go outside of God to get something that could be found in Him the whole time, and to much higher levels!

The enemy still uses this tactic with us today, causing us to look outside of God for the very things that can only truly be found in HIM! We begin chasing temporary fulfillment in titles, positions, relationships etc..when all we truly need can be found in Jesus.

Have you ever been in a season or situation where God told you not to do something, but in your own mind you thought or felt like it was a good thing? Sometimes we may look at things like this and think that God is just really strict as a Father and we may have some rebellion in us that says "is not that bad." Two vital things we need in our true identity are trust and understanding.

We must trust that God knows what is best for us, so that we can let go of the reigns and surrender to His ways.And this doesn't always happen, bit it's also helpful to understand the why behind God's rules.. I'll give you a hint, it's not because He's angry or controlling. It's not because He doesn't want you to have the things your heart desires. When we understand and acknowledge that God has wisdom far beyond what we do , we can trust that he knows what's up ahead. He knows what's inside of us that we might not even realize and he knows what we can actually handle. Far too often we get prideful and think we can handle things that could actually destroy us.

Growing up in a religious home, there were a lot of rules and things I was told that I couldn't do that were sinful- but In my naivety, I thought that these things were actually fun and that God didn't want me to have fun. What I didn't understand is the reason behind why God hates sin. He hates sin because it breaks our hearts. It causes separation between him and us because he is perfect and he cannot be in the presence of sin. But He desires a close relationship with us.

Sin often looks appealing just like the fruit that Eve looked at and she saw that it was "good for food and pleasing to the Eye" sin is this way- it looks fun, it looks pleasing to the Eye, and we think that it will satisfy something inside of us, but what actually ends up happening is, we are suddenly overcome with shame and hide ourselves from God and we separate ourselves from him. Sin makes false promises to fulfill something inside of us that it first tells us we are lacking- but remember- in Him we lack no good thing. When God warned Adam and Eve not to eat the fruit He explained to them that the day that they would eat it they would surely die. Although they didn't drop dead physically when they sinned, a part of them died. Their spirit inside of them died. When things are dead their eyes are closed so when their spirit died their spiritual eyes were closed and their physical senses were heightened, just like a blind person has heightened hearing -when one of your senses is removed the others are heightened. They suddenly recognized their nakedness and were full of shame. Another beautiful attribute that we see in this story is that God comes looking for them because he desires that close relationship with them just as he does with us. But when sin and shame separates, he comes looking for us. God, in his kindness already knew what had happened but he asked the simple question: "who told you that you were naked?" moments ago they were walking in their original design or imago dei and now sin has robbed them of their identity. And as a result, all of mankind is now born into this world incomplete, we grow up learning how to function in ⅔ of who we were actually created to be- physical body and our soul (mind, will and emotions) which leads us down a path of fulfilling our own desires, chasing things that we can see, and may make us feel good momentarily, but can never fill the void. These things often lead to heartbreak. when we look for love in all the wrong places, we end up broken and scarred, this is why God hates sin..He doesn't want His children hurting and broken! This is a clear picture that shows what we believe about ourselves and God, changes the way we act.

So my question to you is who told you that you weren't enough? That you were unlovable, that you were rejected, that you have nothing to offer, that you're not smart enough, not pretty enough: whatever those things are that repeat in your mind who told you? In today's world we're overloaded with ads and information, influencers telling us that we need this or that to make us happy or if we just had that six pack or took this course then I could do what I'm meant to do, and when we're in this fragile state of questioning who we are we will fall for it hook line and sinker.

There is a quote by Penelope Douglas that is a favorite of mine, it says "*we all eat lies when our hearts are hungry.*"

We are all hungry for love and acceptance, God created us as 3 in 1, but part of us is missing..our spirit man is still dead until we come to Him and we are Born Again. (**John 3:1-21**) So often we try to mold and shape ourselves into something that we were never meant to be in order to fit in and feel accepted, but what if you were never meant to fit in.. what if you were meant to stand out!

Remember how I told you that God created the exact space for you before you were created? There is a perfect shaped space exactly created for you that you are meant to take up. Like puzzle pieces that all have a distinct shape and only fit where they are meant to, stop trying to squeeze in to a smaller space, Stop shrinking yourself to fit in. You're not meant to look like someone else, you're not meant to act like someone else, you were created uniquely for a purpose that only you can fulfill. Think about that, if you're changing yourself to fit in, then those people aren't really accepting the real you..they're accepting the fake version of you, which means they're not accepting you at all.

Just like God created Adam and Eve, he created you exactly how you were meant to be down to the very last detail. Don't let the enemy's lies rob you of that fact. Take some time today and evaluate not only what lies you've been believing, but where they have come from. Take a journey through your past and look at the things flooding your time and your mind. If you need to unfollow certain social media accounts because they are leaving you feeling less than or in any way not building you up, let them go. If there is a relationship in your life that makes you change yourself to be accepted, let it go. We must create boundaries for what we allow in our minds and hearts and replace those lies with truth. In order to identify a lie we must first know the truth. The truth isn't just whatever sounds good to you or sounds right ,the world will tell you that truth is subjective and I have my truth and you have your truth but that is not what God says- the truth is objective. Believing in something doesn't make it truth it just means that you believe a lie. The truth is found in God and in his word.

John 14:6 Jesus said, I am the Way the Truth and the Life, no one comes to the Father but through me.

John 8:31- 32 so Jesus said to the Jews who had believed him, "if you abide in my word you are truly my disciples and you will know the truth and the truth will set you free."

Romans 12:2 Do not be conformed to the pattern of this world but be transformed by the renewing of your mind that you may prove what is good and acceptable and perfect will of God.

In order to renew our mind we must first take inventory of what is taking up space in it and remove anything that does not serve us or the purpose God has for us.

Whatever is true, noble ,right, pure, lovely ,admirable, excellent or praiseworthy think about such things Phillippians 4:8

On the next page write out what the specific lies are and confront or oppose them directly with God's truth. Here are a few verses to help you get started.

HE SAYS I AM:

- MASTERPIECE- EPHESIANS 2:10
- ....
- FEARFULLY AND WONDERFULLY MADE- PSALM 139:14
- ....
- A NEW CREATION-2 CORINTHIANS 5:17
- ....
- ORIGINAL- PSALM 139:15-16
- ....
- MADE FOR A PURPOSE- 1 PETER 2:9

LIES
WHAT LIES HAVE I BELIEVED ABOUT MYSELF?

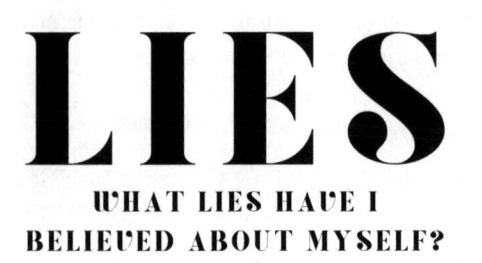

TRUTH

WHO DOES GOD SAY THAT I AM?

CHAPTER 2
Tangled

Chapter 2
Tangled

Now that we have a list of some of the lies we believe we're going to take a closer look, I know you're all eager to get over talking about them and I don't want to dwell on them and allow them any more time or power in your heart and mind but we've got some tending to do
..acknowledging that they're there is just the first step.

We're going to continue looking at the story of Adam and Eve. In Genesis chapter 3 we know that God has confronted Adam and Eve and as a result of their sin; they are now subject to the consequences of their actions and as such there are curses attached. I want to focus on 2 in this book.

Genesis 3:17-18 and to Adam he said because you have listened to the voice of your wife and have eaten of the tree of which I commanded you, you shall not eat of it. cursed is the ground because of you. In pain you shall eat of it all the days of your life, thorns and thistles it shall bring forth for you and you shall eat the plants of the field.

Since I believe the majority of the people reading this book are women I'm going to take a quick detour and speak specifically to women about marriage/relationships. Part of the sin for Adam was that he listened to the voice of his wife over the voice of God. When confronted with this sin he tried to blame Eve but in the end it was his decision- he was the leader of their family. As women there is a saying that the man is the head of the home but the woman is the neck and she can turn the head in any which way she wants. This may seem funny at first glance but this saying is true and it comes with a huge responsibility for us as women in any relationship to always point our men to Jesus. It doesn't matter if we think we know what God wants for our family, we have to point him to Jesus so that God can speak directly to him what he needs to do. And don't get upset if it's the opposite of what you think is best. It's easy for us as women to just say what needs to be done but we have to humble ourselves and submit ourselves to our husbands and to the highest authority- God. This is the order he established. I believe this passage is proof that when a man loves a woman he wants to do what pleases her so much, he may go against what God says just to appease her. In the moment that may seem sweet, but this is wrong and dangerous. We must not take advantage of our men in this way just to have what we want. In the end God knows what's best for us and we must not lean on our own understanding. Ultimately it was Adam's sin that caused the fall of mankind, and the curse fell on all of us because of him. So if we lead our men in the wrong direction rather than pointing him to God we can cause a curse to fall on him and the rest of our family. The goal is not to control him, but to champion him to succeed in leading your family in God's will. It isn't uncommon for God to speak something to you before he tells your husband, but I believe this may be because it takes us time to plan and prepare for these things..take it to Him in prayer and wait for Him to tell your husband Himself..things will go much smoother. This is what God's plan and order looks like in a marriage, if your husband isn't following Him yet, continue to pray that God will do what He does and get ahold of him. And if you're not married yet, may this be a lesson in what to look for when that time comes.

In the verses I mentioned earlier we see that part of the curse were thorns and thistles. Im reminded of growing up having these pesky weeds in our yard that had what we called "goat heads" or "jack stickers" If you know anything about these plants you know how hard they are to get rid of. They often grow low to the ground but their branches spread far and wide, covering as much ground as possible. They tangle themselves around each other and they stick themselves deep into whatever they can grab onto. These prickly thorn like stickers would cling to your pants, socks, shoes..whatever they could..which only spread their seeds even further! Imagine your life is a garden and those lies that you mentioned on the previous pages are thorns and they stick to anything they can and when you try to uproot them they cause pain.

This is often the reason why we leave them alone because we don't want to cause ourselves pain. But you cannot leave a thorn inside of you and expect to heal. If you've ever had a splinter you know how even though it's under the surface every time something brushes up against it you pull away, it hurts. If you leave it there you can adjust your way of life in order not to brush up against it, but we aren't operating in our full capacity. In our spiritual and emotional lives you might call these "triggers" When someone says something or does something that reminds you of someone, maybe it's a smell or a taste that brings back a bad memory and because you never fully healed from that thing it will cause you to have flashbacks, it will trigger you into old mindsets, it can even bring you back to that exact traumatic moment in your life emotionally. This is a sign that you have a thorn or thistle in your life. We must be careful, because this can cause us to get into a cycle of controlling everything and everyone around us to keep ourselves protected. If you think about wounds under the surface that are unhealed, they fester, they will spread and get infected then they affect other parts of your life. Have you ever had a person in your life that for some unknown reason you couldn't stand them? Sure, everyone has different taste in personalities etc, but sometimes this can be a sign for you to look closer. What is it about them you don't like? Do they remind you of someone else that you have past issues with? You may have a splinter. The enemy loves to keep you in these cycles of control,and avoiding certain people, coddling your trauma to keep it hushed, all the while evil spirits are comfy cozy deep inside. Your "self protection" is more likely "self preservation" and we aren't called to preserve self, we are called to die to self.

If even the thought of going back and looking at these traumatic events in your life makes you cringe and want to stop right here, remember, the enemy will have you thinking that if you just cover it up you don't have to worry about it, out of sight out of mind right? He doesn't want you healed, because your broken self provides a great environment for his work in your life. He offers plenty of other options of temporary numbing through substances, relationships, busyness etc. all the while you're being held captive. But don't let the thought of exposing them make you afraid, an enemy exposed, is an enemy defeated! God is the ultimate healer and he isn't interested in just cleaning up the surface. He wants to go deeper to the root of the issue

open it up, and expose it for what it truly is so that you can fully and completely heal -He will not put bandaids on bullet holes. And when you are healed, you won't continue to bleed on other people..you'll be able to help them heal too! This isn't a quick process either.. it takes time to get through the layers, don't rush it.

In the beginning stages of my journey of uprooting lies a song had come out by Tasha Layton called "Look what you've done" I would play it on repeat as I wrote down all the lies I believed about myself. I pictured these roots all around me tangled together like a cage, keeping me from moving into what I felt I was supposed to. I just knew deep in my spirit that the life I was living in wasn't all that God had for me and it made me restless.

My favorite lyrics from the song say " You spoke your truth into the lies I let my heart believe" and there is the key..the Truth of God's word and who He says I am is the standard that I must compare every other thought to. If you can, take a few minutes and listen to this song..let the lyrics sink in. The enemy wants us stuck in this cage of thorns unable to move..but Jesus died to set us free from that! What Jesus did on the cross nullifies what we have done in God's eyes. You may have tried in the past to get rid of these things and only chopped off the top of the weed, but we must go to the source to stop it from growing back.

YOUR "SELF PROTECTION" IS MORE LIKELY "SELF PRESERVATION" AND WE AREN'T CALLED TO PRESERVE SELF, WE ARE CALLED TO DIE TO SELF.

Once we have removed the lies we can sometimes feel empty, raw and unsure of what to do next or who we are. Bits of our identity may have been attached to those things and we find ourselves disoriented. I know in my own journey, I had a root of rejection that I never knew was there, it had come to me in the womb..and when God exposed it and removed it I felt a huge empty space inside, it felt like that root must have been 10 feet wide. But just like with soil in nature, if you remove something without planting something new in its place, the next time it rains all the nutrients from the soil wash away. But good things require those nutrients to grow.

This reminds me of a short story in the Bible **Matthew 12:43-45** that talks about an unclean spirit (demon) who has left its home and is wandering looking for a new one..when it finds none it returns to where it came from to find it clean, swept and in order and brings back 7 more spirits worse than itself. And the person is worse off than before. Now I don't share this story to scare you (there's a whole chapter dedicated to fear coming up) but to make you aware.

This is a perfect example of what it looks like to uproot things, clean house and not plant anything new..God's word tells us its only a matter of time until the enemy comes to plant new seeds in those empty spaces to get you back in bondage. Unclean spirits only require an empty shell to inhabit..they're not too picky about their environment..the darker the better. So we MUST immediately ask the Holy Spirit to fill us back up..to plant the seeds He intended us to cultivate and grow in those places. But like most things with God, we have a part too..we must take action. When those old thought patterns start coming back up, we must take them captive and replace them with Truth. Plant the seeds He's given you, so you don't leave room for more evil to enter!

JOHN 8:31-32 **I**F YOU ABIDE IN MY WORD, YOU ARE TRULY MY DISCIPLES, AND YOU WILL KNOW THE TRUTH AND THE TRUTH WILL SET YOU FREE.

JOHN 14:6 **I** AM THE WAY, THE TRUTH, AND THE LIFE.

JOHN 8:36 **S**O IF THE **S**ON SETS YOU FREE, YOU WILL BE FREE INDEED.

This is how we protect our mind and heart..we abide in Jesus and allow His Truth to fill us. Open yourself up to Him, so that He can come in and dig those roots up and burn them with Holy fire so they never return. We already took time to write down the lies..so I want you to take time and ask God to quiet every voice but His, and show you how He sees you..write down what you hear.

In God's original design there was never meant to be thorns and thistles, this is a result of sin, but Jesus came to save us from the curse and bring us back to our original design. When we accept the sacrifice He made on the cross as payment for our sin, we are restored to communion with Him. Even though we still live in a fallen world and people around us still live with these things and have even accepted them as part of life, we dont have to do that when we've been born again into God's family. As children of the King of Kings we have an inheritance that includes dominion and authority over the enemy! HALLELUJAH!

When God took me through this process I Imagined myself tangled up in roots that had been growing deep in the soil of my family and passed down to me. I didn't always have the choice of what traumas and circumstances I was involved in, but I was trapped by them mentally and spiritually like a prisoner. I recognized thought patterns I had that I knew my mother also struggled with. Thoughts of insecurity and self consciousnes, anxiety, etc. These are often things we just asssume are normal in life because they are common. But I submit to you that much like those weeds that grow far and wide on the ground, these thoughts and patterns grow far and wide in our bloodlines and can keep us from achieving the very things God desires for our lives. That's exactly what the enemy wants. But God desires to set us free from those very things!

It's not a coincidence that when Jesus went to the cross He bore a crown of thorns on His head. To me this signifies the mental thorns that wrap themselves around our minds, and that Jesus bore that for us too. The price for our sins, and our struggles was already paid for on the cross, so that we could be set free from those things..but in the same way that one cannot receive salvation, even though it's been paid for by Christ, until we ask for it, we must also ask the Lord to set us free from everything that hinders us. Ask Him to reveal to us the wrong thinking and mindsets we've had and to set us free. Jesus death on the cross wasn't just so we could receive salvation, but for every curse that was laid out in the beginning when Adam sinned. The crown of thorns, the 39 stripes on His back, the spear in His side, all have purpose and deeper meaning behind them. They were a physical representation of what Jesus was redeeming us from.

Let's talk a little more about planting good things in our lives. Have you ever had a dream or vision for your future? These are some of the seeds we are given. .they are the baby version of something that God may have planted in you long ago, it is our responsibility to steward these seeds, to cultivate, water and help them grow into fruit in our lives, but while the seed is growing, first underground, then sprouting and getting taller and more mature- so are we! You see God is such a good Father that He won't give us gifts that we cant carry. Imagine giving a 5 year old a million dollars..they would probably buy silly things like candy and toys because they aren't mature enough to steward it well. The same goes for us, sometimes we think we're ready for that thing God planted in us to come, but He knows if we had it now it would destroy us. Believe me, I know how frustrating it can be to know what God wants you to do in life and have no clue how to do it or to feel like you've done all you can but it still isn't happening yet. But when we trust God, we have to also trust His timing and know that He must know something that we don't yet. Everything He does has a purpose.
There is a quote that I love that says this:

For a seed to achieve its greatest expression it must come completely undone. The shell cracks, its insides come out and everything changes to someone who doesn't understand growth. It would look a lot like destruction.
Cynthia Occelli

I love this so much because it is in the undoing of ourselves and who we think we are that we can discover who we were always meant to be!

When you think about your life this doesn't sound like a fun part of the process but this is a vitally important part of it because there may be times when you feel like you're falling apart and nothing is working out right and it can be tempting to just give up, but you'll never reap the harvest if you don't do the work. Every seed has a time attached to it ..when it's planted in good soil it's only a matter of TIME.
Think about a farmer, if he were to plant an entire field of crops and got upset that the next day he didn't have full grown,ready to harvest crops and just decided to burn it all down he would never have any food. We cannot give up on our dreams just because they take time to develop. Remember, the enemy wants us focused on what we can see physically,and keep us blinded spiritually to what God is doing in this process. We must choose to have faith in Him,even when we cannot see.

Ecclesiastes 11:6 in the morning sow your seed and evening let your hands not be idle for you do not know which will succeed whether this or that or whether both will do equally well.

Ecclesiastes 3:1 2 For everything there is a season, a time for every activity under heaven, a time to be born and a time to die, a time to plant and a time to harvest.

Galatians 6:9 So let's not get tired of doing what is good at just the right time; we will reap a harvest of blessing if we don't give up.

John 12:24 Truly, truly, I say to you, unless a grain of wheat falls into the earth and dies, it remains alone; but if it dies, it bears much fruit.

We have a choice of what to do with the seeds God has given us. Sometimes we may be too afraid to even plant them. Planting requires faith that God will provide rain and all the things we need for it to grow. Faith is believing in what we cannot see. I want to say a quick prayer over you as you reflect over these roots and sowing new seeds.

Lord, I come to you today and I ask that you expose the enemies' schemes, reveal the thorns that have dug themselves so deep in our lives, some that even run through the generations. Give us the courage to push forward in the process and know that you are a good Father, and you do everything for our good. I ask that you would rip them out by the root and destroy them in your Holy fire, break us free from the limitations they have set and give us your boundless grace and freedom. I ask you Holy Spirit to come in like a flood and fill in every space from the top of the head to the soles of the feet, body, soul and spirit, Lord. I ask that you would heal the wounds that are left behind and give us rest, give us clarity and fresh vision for what you want us to do in our lives and help us to plant the seeds we've been given and steward them well. Thank you for the sacrifice you've made to bring us back into a right relationship with you and help us to walk in that freedom and obedience to you. Amen.

CHAPTER 3
LOVED

Chapter 3
Loved

I want to take this entire chapter to cultivate in you something that I believe will hold one of the deepest, strongest roots that is needed in our lives for stability in the future and that is love.

In a world where everyone is constantly aching to feel accepted and loved and social media is handing out false advertisements promising to keep us connected, why is it that we can feel more disconnected, unheard, unseen and unloved than ever ? I think we all know by now that the lives that people pretend to have and post are not a true reflection of reality, but when we find ourselves hungering for connection it's easy to grab our phones and scroll endlessly into oblivion and many times we may feel worse about ourselves afterward or look at our families and feel less connected to who matters most.

What if you felt loved and seen for who you truly are, everything you see as a flaw was cherished? Then you wouldn't be settling for scraps of attention from others or maybe you would have a bigger capacity to love those right around you a little better.

1 THESSALONIANS 3:12 MAY THE LORD MAKE YOUR LOVE INCREASE AND OVERFLOW FOR EACH OTHER AND EVERYONE ELSE JUST AS OURS DOES FOR YOU.

ROMANS 8:38-39 FOR I AM CONVINCED THAT NEITHER DEATH NOR LIFE NEITHER ANGELS NOR DEMONS NEITHER PRESENT NOR FUTURE NOR ANY POWERS NEITHER HEIGHT NOR DEPTH OR ANYTHING ELSE IN ALL CREATION CAN SEPARATE US FROM THE LOVE OF GOD THAT IS IN CHRIST JESUS OUR LORD.

EPHESIANS 3:17-19 MAY YOUR ROOTS GO DOWN DEEP INTO THE SOIL OF GOD'S MARVELOUS LOVE AND MAY YOU HAVE THE POWER TO UNDERSTAND AS ALL GOD'S PEOPLE SHOULD, HOW WIDE, HOW LONG, HOW HIGH AND HOW DEEP HIS LOVE REALLY IS.

This verse above tells us that God's love is the soil in which we plant..I didn't realize until I was an adult that this particular thing that I needed was so important. Love matters, it is woven into the core of our being we need to love and be loved. And I'd like to share a personal story with you of a time God planted a seed in me that shook me and it has taken root deep in my heart and spirit.

After having a seaon of my marriage where my husband and I were separated,on the verge of divorce, we had come to a point where God restored our family. My husband gave his life to Christ and things were looking up. I had finally become a hairstylist like I'd always dreamed of, we bought a house with land, my husband started his own business also. But 1.5 years after opening my own salon suite the Lord spoke to me one evening on my way to work. As I walked in the door I felt this deep sense that I would not be coming there much longer. So many questions came to my mind, and I couldnt explain it but I just knew my time there was short. As months passed by He confirmed and clarified that He was asking me to lay down this dream of mine, for His dream for my life. That may seem like a no brainer, but it was a difficult decision that I knew would impact our whole family, and having just come out of a long hard season in my marriage I was not too sure I was ready for more difficulty. It took alot of prayer, confirmations and time but I made the descision to do so..at first I was excited to see what else God had in store for me, because I knew He had something in mind. I thought it would happen fairly quickly and I would go from closing my salon straight into his mission..but I was wrong. Instead, the Lord led me into a season of hiddenness. And it was extremely uncomfortable.

You see, I grew up in a home where we weren't really celebrated or praised unless we did something good (usually for the church) So even though I know now that my parents always loved me regardless, as a child I mistook this attention for love and this began a pattern of feeling like I always had to do something in order to be valuable or loved. This performance mindset followed me into adulthood, relationships, jobs, churches etc. I always knew I had to use my gifts for God, so in my mind that meant I would talk about Jesus, serve in the church and anytime someone praised me for it I would give God the glory, and that's all well and good.. but God knew my heart wasn't in the right place..I was striving for acceptance, approval and love from others and from God.. not realizing I already had it long before I ever lifted a finger. But in this particular season, I wasn't using any of my gifts, and when I did try to use them I wasn't getting much praise for it, I had door after door closed in my face when I would attempt to serve even in my church and I didn't know why. I felt like I was failing. I thought "God how am I supposed to please you if you won't let me do anything!? "

Then one day in a state of desperation, lying in bed feeling so unfulfilled with my life, questioning if I did the right thing by closing my salon, I was scrolling through my phone and came across a sermon that piqued my interest. And as I listened to the message Holy Spirit began to reveal His heart toward me and it wrecked me.

The pastor was speaking about how God loves each and every one of us, in his story he gave the example of a child who has a stuffed animal or a blanky or some item that they love and cherish and have to take with them everywhere. They often are ratty, dirty, torn and stinky but to that child it means the world. They can't go to sleep without it, or leave the house unless this object is in tow It's a necessity to them and although it may not be important to anyone else or may not be worth a lot of money -to that child it means everything. If you have been around a child like this, you know their entire world can come crashing down without this thing.

As I listened to this message I was reminded of a bear that I had when I was young. A panda bear, I still own to this day. His dingy white and black fur is matted from all the times it's been washed, his little nose is colored on with a black sharpie because the button fell off at some point, and on its back it had a music box that you could twist the dial and it would play the song "Jesus loves me." I remember many nights waking up afraid from a nightmare, in my bed alone and I would turn the dial to listen to that tune and my fear would go away as I sang the song in my head and even sometimes out loud. As those memories replayed in my mind I began to cry as God specifically told me that even in those times as a young child when I was afraid that little bear was telling me that Jesus loved me,I realized that throughout my entire life Jesus has been telling me that he loves me, even when I was doing the wrong things, or doing nothing at all . The simple things we think in childhood are just part of a religion or tradition to sing songs and quote verses and things truly do have meaning behind them. And even many years later can have a huge impact on our lives. I have a new love and appreciation for the song, because of this.

During this season of hiding there was no one to see my good works, or praise me for things..and God was teaching me that there were roots that He was exposing and removing in me, and at the same time showing me how He had planted seeds of love all along my lifetime. I questioned what was going on in my life and why things didn't seem to be the way I thought they should be and sometimes I felt like I had done everything I was supposed to do to please God and yet he wasn't speaking and he wasn't changing my circumstances and I felt like He wasn't around. But in these moments where I seemed to be unnoticed and unappreciated, He reminded me with that memory of my bear that He's always been there, And he has always loved me. Not because of what I could do for him but just because I am His! Even as an infant before I could really do much at all for God he loved me then. Unlike people, God's love is not conditional, it is not based on our performance. It's not because of who we are or what we have accomplished or the gifts we have and how well we use them for him, His love is there because we belong to Him. The Bible says that He delights in us. (Psalm 18) How amazing is that!?

This is what it looked like in my life to come undone, and Im thankful now that I was hidden at that time so no one else had to see me that way. But when we come undone in Him, all His love can then get inside of us and helps us to absorb the nutrients we need to continue growing healthily.

Think of that child who has lost his stuffed animal or blanky or whatever that special object is and how distraught he is when he can't find it and the joy that overtakes him when he finds it. We bring God that kind of joy! There are countless stories in the Bible that talk about Jesus's love for us and we know that He loved us so much that He sent Jesus to die for us, But sometimes we can brush these off as just old traditions or stories that we've heard a million times but the message in them is still just as true as it was the day that He did it.

We must allow this message to go from being in our mind to being deeply rooted in our hearts. Remember it's the soil, it must be cultivated to grow good things..and from there we can live FROM love instead of FOR love. From the very moment that sin separated man from God He made a plan to bridge that gap because He loves us so much He doesn't want to live without us for eternity. And he knew that the only way that we could be with him forever was to become the sacrifice himself, He moved heaven and Earth,came down from his throne to be that sacrifice. As he hung on the cross with his arms stretched wide, one arm reaching from heaven and the other arm reaching for us He became the bridge.

Sometimes it's difficult for us to believe things in our hearts because we think of God as some man in the sky who is far away and not near and we may not have developed a close personal relationship with the Holy Spirit yet. I'd like to help you understand this and drive it in a little deeper and hopefully help you understand how personal this really is. The Bible is literally a love letter to us!

❛❜❛❜

Consider this:

In Jewish tradition A father would choose a bride for his son. He would have to pay a "bride price" for her to her father, which was very expensive. This price was a symbol of how much he loved her. When both parties agreed, they were "betrothed" or engaged and would seal the agreement celebrating with wine (this is where we see the last supper in **Luke 22:19-20**) Jesus referred to the wine as His blood, in this tradition the woman would reject the proposal by pushing away the cup or accepting it by drinking the wine..this paints a picture of where mankind is right now...Jesus has offered his payment and proposal for us to accept or reject. If she accepted they would not live together or consummate the marriage yet, but the woman would then wear a head covering to signify she was "set apart" and spoken for. Everyone would know clearly she was different.

The engaged couple would remain living with their parents and the groom would go back to prepare a place for his bride. (**John 14:3**) He would build an addition onto his father's house, sometimes this took over a year! When the father saw that it was acceptable, he would tell his son he could go get His bride, but neither the bride or the groom knew when this would happen. Oh the suspense! In the Bible, believers are called the "Bride of Christ" and Jesus is the Groom. Before Jesus left this earth, He paid the price for us, the highest price of all- His life! And He told His disciples He was going to prepare a place for us in his father's house. But that he would return one day and that no one would know the day or the hour that he will come, only the father knows. (**Matthew 24:36**) So as the bride of Christ we wait in suspense for His return to come and take us away so that we can have the marriage supper and so that we can fully become one flesh with Him, and live together for all eternity!

I don't know about you but the most personal relationship I can think of in the world is that of a marriage. In marriage you know someone so well, you know their flaws, you know their quirks, you know their strengths and weaknesses, And even though sometimes we don't always get along or see eye to eye, we choose to stay, we choose to love regardless. You see, true love is not an emotion that goes up-and-down like a roller coaster, its not something you just fall into or out of..true love is a choice that we make every single day. Marriage is a covenant that says no matter what I'm here, I'm not backing out, there is no backup plan- you're it. And even if you aren't married or maybe your marriage didnt work out this way, people can let us down, but Jesus never will. You see God isn't after anything that we can do for him he's just after our hearts. He wants us to know just how much he loves us.

One of my favorite words in scripture is HESED. This word is so rich there is no English equivalent to it. It encompasses things like mercy, steadfast love, favor goodness, loyalty, loving-kindness and is most closely associated with grace. Often used to display the covenant love God has for Israel, a love that will not let them go. Israel consistently turned away from a God who loves them but we see that he relentlessly chases after them, and pursues them time and time again. This word means that he has bound himself to his own -that's you and me! It's a kind of love that stays no matter what. It is permanent, enduring and constant. This is God's character!

Jeremiah 31:3 I have loved you with an everlasting love. I have drawn you with unfailing kindness.

This type of love is echoed all throughout scripture and I'm reminded of the story in the Gospels where the shepherd leaves the 99 for the one lost sheep. (**Luke 15:4-7**) We are also referred to as sheep, which are not the smartest animals; they often wander off into dangerous places and find themselves stuck. Sheep are safest in a flock and close to the shepherd. The Bible calls Jesus The Good Shepherd. Sometimes shepherds will come together and let their flocks graze together or even pen them in a sheep fold together. But each shepherd has a distinct sound or signal that only his sheep recognize and follow..Scripture says "my sheep hear my voice, I know them and they follow me." (**John 10:27-28**) so even in a world where were bombarded with noise and distraction, when God speaks even in a whisper, we can recognize it. .but we have to spend time in His presence and listening to Him to get used to it. What good is any relationship without communication?

One of my biggest frustrations in my Christian walk used to be that I was always told to ask God for direction etc, and I didn't know yet how to do that. .I knew I needed to read my Bible and pray but even when I did that I didn't seem to hear His voice as much as I wanted or I would question if it was really Him I was hearing, and it was discouraging..I knew I must be missing something! But that desire to hear Him more, took me on a journey to discover what I was missing, and He met me there. I had been saved and baptized, yes, but I didn't know that I should pray before reading scripture and ask the Holy Spirit to speak to me, teach me what He wanted me to know and open my eyes and heart to recieve it. If you are in a similar place of frustration feeling like you're doing the things but not getting the revelation you desire, try praying that next time. Holy Spirit is an essential part of life for a believer. It's not a coincidence that scripture often refers to Him as the Living Water (**John 7:38**) and Breath of Life. **(Genesis 2:7)
(John 20:19-23)**

To take this a step further, another thing I came to know is the baptism in the Holy Spirit. I was never taught about it growing up Southern Baptist, so this concept was completely new to me, but it is clearly in scripture. After Jesus resurrection, (**Luke 24:49**)(**Acts 1**) He told his disciples that they should wait in Jerusalem and He kept promising a helper to be with them even after he left ,this is where we find the story of penacost.(**Acts 2:1-13**) One day in the upper room as Jesus's followers were waiting for what he had promised a mighty wind came rushing in and suddenly there were tongues of fire resting on each of them and they began speaking in tongues that weren't their own and they came outside and people accuse them of being drunk but then they realized that the language they were speaking was actually their language! How could this be? They were from a different country and they didn't know how they knew their language. But they were speaking about God and about Jesus and what he had done -they were prophesying of the Messiah! This was when the Holy Spirit came upon them and gave them supernatural power to speak in other languages, they had the fire of the Holy Spirit dwelling in them. In the Old Testament we see fire as a symbol of the Holy Spirit with Moses and the burning Bush and in the wilderness and the tabernacle etc, but now in the New Testament this fire has come to dwell in his followers and it gives them power. This did not stop with just these people, this wasn't a one time outpouring- this is something that we can take advantage of even today! The Bible says that even in the last days He will pour out his spirit upon his sons and daughters and they will prophesy and they will have visions and dream dreams.(**Acts 2:17**) That is us! We are in the last days as the bride of Christ. We are awaiting his imminent return ,but He gave us a helper to get through until then. To help us to be witnesses, to give us boldness, to give us the ability to speak in languages that we don't know, to prophesy of Him. To be able to lay hands-on people and see them healed, To take authority over evil spirits and demons and cast them out just like Jesus and the disciples did in those days- we have that same ability. The Bible clearly says that when we accept Jesus into our hearts we receive the Holy Spirit. He is in us, we are the temple of the Holy Spirit. But this separate baptism in the Holy Spirit means to be immersed in Him so now not only does he live in us but we live in him. (**Acts 1:8**) This is the baptism of fire that is spoken about. And it is only through the work of the Holy Spirit that people come to know Jesus and their lives are changed. God loves and accepts us as we are, but He desires to make us new, help us grow and see our potential, so He doesn't leave us the same way He found us. Transformation is inevitable in His presence! Holy Spirit will give you the ability to see beyond the physical words on the page and show you more! (**Jeremiah 33:3**)

Take some time to pray and read the scriptures listed in this chapter for yourself. Even if you've read them all before, ask Holy Spirit to reveal something new to you! God's word is alive and active, and He is so vast we can never know everything about Him, there's always more! I pray that this time spent with Him will reveal just how loved you truly are by God!

CHAPTER 4
FEARLESS

Chapter 1
Fearless

Allowing God to peel back the layers of identity we've put on and adopted over the course of our lives can be painful, it makes you feel exposed, vulnerable and raw. It can make you feel lost, like, what's left of me God? I thought you loved me for me? Why do I have to be completely undone? But look deeper at what He is doing in this process.. He is removing the things that were never meant to fulfill you. Yes, some of the roles and things you have done are good and part of His plan for you, but they were never meant to become you. As humans we often ask what occupation someone has, or who they're related to, in an effort to get to know them better. And while we may be able to identify them as so and so's mom or sister, that's not their identity. These days many people "identify" as a certain gender, or animal, or adopt traits or diagnosis' as part of their identity such as introvert/ extrovert, ADHD, etc. . Which again are not identity. What this book is not meant to do is add to the identity crisis we have in society where people are so lost about who they are that we just decide they can be whoever or whatever they feel like in the moment and if you don't not only accept , but affirm that decision, you're suddenly an intolerant bigot.

Being undone by God is never a bad thing, even if it feels scary.. because He always finishes what He starts! He never tears down without rebuilding.. Jesus was a carpenter afterall. .a craftsman, who chose dust of all things to create man out of. So if you are in a place in your life where you feel like you've fallen so far apart you can't even glue the pieces back together.. you're in good hands! Sometimes it's helpful rather than trying to come up with "who am I?" Is to establish who you aren't. Sort of a process of elimination. I'd like to share a personal testimony of something that I had my entire life that I truly just accepted as who I was, and later God revealed to me it wasn't conducive of who He created me to be.

For as long as I can remember I struggled with fear. I remember being afraid of the dark as a kid and always having nightmares, I used to be afraid of the silliest things like the 7Up commercial character, and bigfoot. I remember always needing my mom to come on school field trips and even in 3rd grade would get sick to my stomach everyday before going to school. I had a lifelong fear of being kidnapped even into adulthood. I would constantly be looking behind me at stores and hated being in big crowds. Now, don't get me wrong I believe there is a healthy amount of awareness that we should all have of our surroundings, but this went far beyond rational. But that's what fear does isnt it? It causes you to live in a state of "what if?" I know fear isn't always the word we like to use, now we usually call it anxiety..but even worry is a form of fear.

There was a verse I used to sing as a kid to help calm me, it says **"God did not give us a spirit of fear, but of Power, love and a sound mind" 2Timothy 1:7** What I came to learn as I grew in my walk with God is this verse tells us that fear is a spirit, not only that, but one that God didnt give us! And God told me this particular spirit was passed down to me from my mother, and that He wanted to end this anxiety in my life and deliver me from that spirit. And He did just that!

But these days people take these spirits, such as anxiety, depression, etc as part of their identity. The enemy wants to keep us in fear and bondage to these things and just accept them or even find other people with the same issues to accept us or medicating to find relief.

But if you continue reading in 2 Timothy Paul is telling his friend to boldy share the gospel and not fear. He tells him that they have been delivered, saved and called or 'set apart' for a special purpose. And we also have a special purpose! None of us was created by accident. But the enemy doesn't want us to see that.. and so he uses spirits, such as fear to keep us from moving forward in what God has for us to do. As for me the fear I had as a kid might seem like it's totally normal and most kids have some of that, but as I mentioned, it was passed down from my mom.. and I have discovered that fear had such a grip on me because of my calling. The enemy isn't dumb, he is very purposeful in his attacks and I know that he will use specific spirits that oppose your specific calling.. so pay close attention to the things you're tempted/ attacked with! I wasn't called to cower in the face of the enemy, I was given power and authority to trample him! (**Luke10:19**) As a child fear may seem harmless and even normal, which is probably why this spirit gets in early in life..but in adulthood it can keep you in bad situations, keep you from going for that new opportunity at work or even the call God has put on your life. Fear can control us, and can also cause us to "control" every situation in our lives so that we can feel safe. There is a short story in (**Mark 4:35-40**) where Jesus and His disciples are on a boat and a storm starts brewing..Jesus is sleeping in the boat and as the storm starts raging, his disciples are questioning how the heck he can sleep through this crazy storm because they are sure they might die! They wake Jesus up and he rebukes the storm and tells it to "Be Still" and it did!

I believe part of the reason he was able to remain calm in the storm is because he knew who he was, he knew that God had a purpose for him and that nothing could stop that from happening. Also consider this physical storm in the story is happening on re of a lake.. this isn't the ocean.. so I believe it is referring to a spiritual storm and can represent storms in our lives, and we can rest assured that God will not Allow anything to destroy us. The enemy loves to keep us distracted by things we can physically see while behind the scenes spiritually there is a battle going on.

What Jesus did in this story when the disciples woke him up is also a great example for us. He rebuked the waves and wind! If God is in control of the elements of the the earth, why would his Son Jesus rebuke them? This is another reason I believe this wasn't just a physical storm, but represents a spiritual one as well. These winds and waves were causing fear in the disciples, which as we know is demonic, and Jesus' verbal rebuke made them cease. The enemy has no actual power over us that we don't allow. The disciples didnt understand that yet, but Jesus did. He understood the power of His words!

Another passage in **Matthew 14:22-33** we see where Jesus walks on the water, and Peter asks him to help him do the same..Peter steps out of the boat when Jesus welcomes him to, but he quickly begins to take his focus off of Jesus and onto the waves..it didnt say there was a storm before, but when he took a step of faith, it came. Peter began to sink and Jesus immediately reaches out and pulls him back up and they get in the boat. I love how Peter was the only one of the disciples to ask to do the seemingly impossible things that Jesus was doing, it shows his faith, even if it was short lived. This is yet another example of Jesus showing His authority over the waves and wind. Things that often overtake us and we begin to sink, can be easily overcome when we understand the authority we have in Christ through the Holy Spirit.

But we get to choose which thoughts we allow to roll around in our minds. Will we decide to focus on the circumstances of life and what we see physically happening around us, or will we put our focus on Jesus who is the author and finisher of our faith? **Hebrews 12:2**

////

The only thing that can keep His plan for our lives from happening is us, because God is a gentleman and will never force his way in our lives. We have a choice of which voices we listen to. I mentioned fear here because that is one of the most common ones and one I dealt with personally but fear can open the door for many other spirits in our lives. When I knew it was time for me to directly engage with the spirit of fear, I was terrified and on the brink of an anxiety attack just thinking about it..that's how this spirit works..it keeps you afraid to make you freeze up and not move forward. But I was able to push through the fear and little did I know, that was just the tip of the iceberg..I had many other spirits inside me and had no idea! But God knew and He wanted to get rid of them and the influence they had in my life. I cant explain everything about deliverance in this book but I will give you a few key things to know. This wasn't something I was taught about growing up and God himself brought me to the right resources to learn about it and help me get free. So here is just the start.

1. Spirits enter through generational curses, trauma and choices/open doors. (Can be passed down from parents such as addictions, abuse or traumatic events and through occult practices by you or family,horror movies/games,ouija boards,crystals,tarot/palm reading etc.)**Exodus 20:5, Exodus 34:7,Numbers 14:18,Leviticus 19:26, Deuteronomy 18:10-12,Leviticus 20:6**

2. Christians can have demons (this is often debated) but the Bible tells us deliverance is the children's bread(**Matthew 15:26**).. and only Christians are children of God. It is part of our inheritance, but Jesus also delivered another woman's daughter in scripture too because of her faith and I believe it led to her salvation. (**Matt 15: 21-28**)

3. Jesus is our deliverer! Throughout the new Testament Jesus cast out many demons from people and so did his disciples, and he gave us this same authority through the Holy Spirit in the name of Jesus. (**John 14:12**) (**John 10:10**) (**psalm 34:17**)(**psalm 34:4**)

It might seem odd that I would talk about deliverance in a book about identity and even in a chapter on fear, but this is exactly how God brought these things to me in my life..and the enemy used my fear of scary things to stay hidden in my life and I could have easily accepted that I, like many other people,and continued to suffer from anxiety..but when God showed me what it truly was and that He had given me authority over it, I was finally set free from that spirit and I dont live with it anymore!

In the process of removing things that are NOT who I truly am, God also taught me about my inheritance and authority as a daughter of the King! Take some time to reflect and ask God to reveal any spirits that you have unknowingly or knowingly allowed into your life and maybe even partnered with and accepted as just who you are.

The first step after identifying these spirits is to repent and renounce (out loud) any/all involvement with these things and close any open doors in your life..this may require you to change the music you listen to, people you hang out with etc..but I can guarantee the freedom is 100 percent worth the sacrifice! You can find many resources online and specific prayers to renounce certain things as well.

Some key things to know are:

- Your relationship with God is where your authority comes from,if you have no relationship,the demons know you have no authority. (**Acts 19**)

- renounce (out loud) any involvement with occult practices/witchcraft,addiction etc from yourself and past generations. This revokes the legal rights for them to be there.

- Repent/confess any sin that He brings to your mind (out loud)

- Forgive those who have caused you trauma (unforgiveness is an open door too!) and forgive yourself-that is often the toughest part.

- Command the spirit(s) to leave in the name of Jesus Christ! If a specific one comes to mind, this is a word of knowledge from Holy Spirit..call it out!

- It is common to yawn,cough,gag, feel the need to scream etc when these spirits are leaving..don't be afraid. Let it go!

- The Holy Spirit is the one who delivers us, but like I mentioned in the previous chapter, when an evil spirit leaves, it may come back and see things cleaned up, and invite 7 more of its friends. So the way we ensure this doesn't happen is to invite Holy Spirit to fill up every empty space left. Spend time in His presence, put on some worship music ("Fill Me Up" by Tasha cobbs is a great option) He will minister to you exactly how He needs to.

- Get connected to a local church/ministry to disciple you further. This is part of filling those empty spaces too. You can cast out a spirit, but if you dont retrain yourself, you can easily fall back into old habits and reopen the door. Accountability is important!

CHAPTER 5
Beyond Compare

Chapter 5
Beyond Compare

"Comparison is a thief of Joy." You may have heard this quote before, but my question is.. has it ever stolen from you? How much has it stolen from you? It's easy to tell people not to compare themselves to others, or to say we don't care what others think about us, but I think for most of us, that would be a lie. From a very young age we learn to compare good/ evil.. but not everything is so black and white. Some of us may have had comparisons at school, or church or even in our own family between siblings or cousins. Have you ever felt the sting of feeling like you didn't quite do things as good as someone else? The problem with this thinking is that we tend to believe that if we don't do it like them, then we must be terrible at it.. rather than celebrating that we are both equally good at something but have different methods. This can go far beyond the typical work/ talent competitive thing and can go to our core of beliefs of who we are. And I believe that the root of comparison comes from a lack mindset. If you think about it, the reason people compete for things in life is because there is usually a limited supply of something, males compete for female mates, teams compete for titles, athletes compete for trophies.. so they must be better than others in order to win right? As humans have tried to give everyone a participation trophy so nobody feels left out or like a loser.. although I see the heart behind that, it also lowers the bar for excellence and has caused other issues.. if everyone wins, then why do we need to put in extra work or practice, right? It has caused a lack of motivation, drive and purpose in people. But neither of these types of thinking work in the Kingdom.. know why? Because there is no lack, and there is no competition. Let me explain.

Let's start with the Lack mindset.

I grew up in a home that didn't have a lot of fancy things, but we always had everything we needed. We may not have gotten every desire we ever had, and I think most of the time we didn't even bother to ask for certain things because we just knew we couldn't afford it. As I became an adult I became more concerned about living a life that I could give myself and my family all the things we wanted. And if I'm honest it was because I wanted to be perceived a certain way to others. I didn't realize it at the time but this gave me the need to "hustle" in order to maintain a certain level of status in my own mind. As I mentioned in a previous chapter, we often compare ourselves to the picture perfect instagram lives that others pretend to have..but the problem is we compare their front with our behind the scenes, and it makes us feel less than desirable.

The problem so many people have these days is that we've lost the ability to be vulnerable and honest with others and even ourselves because we feel the need to look a certain way..we dont want to burden others with our problems or bring them down with us..I know I'm guilty of this! But it is only in honest, humble vulnerability that we can truly be seen and accepted. Our God does not lack anything..He owns the cattle on a thousand hills and paves his streets with asphalt made of gold! What makes you think He can't supply your needs?

PROVERBS 10:3 THE **LORD** DOES NOT LET THE RIGHTEOUS GO HUNGRY,BUT HE THWARTS THE CRAVING OF THE WICKED.

PSALM 33:9-10 OH, FEAR THE **LORD**, YOU HIS SAINTS,FOR THOSE WHO FEAR HIM HAVE NO LACK! THE YOUNG LIONS SUFFER WANT AND HUNGER; BUT THOSE WHO SEEK THE **LORD** LACK NO GOOD THING.

PSALM 37:25 I HAVE BEEN YOUNG, AND NOW AM OLD,YET I HAVE NOT SEEN THE RIGHTEOUS FORSAKEN OR HIS CHILDREN BEGGING FOR BREAD.

MATTHEW 6:33 **B**UT SEEK FIRST THE KINGDOM OF GOD AND HIS RIGHTEOUSNESS, AND ALL THESE THINGS WILL BE ADDED TO YOU.

////

These verses all prove God's character.
But what about ours? What is something that you fear you lack? Where do you find yourself comparing yourself to others and think you fall short? I believe there can be a healthy honesty with ourselves where we can see that we may need to improve in some area, but it should never come from a condemning place or comparing ourselves to others. We can pray and ask the Holy Spirit to teach us how to be more like Him and who He created us to be. He has no limitations, so beauty, talent and gifts are not in short supply, He didn't run out when He came to you. Both flowers and butterflies are beautiful and yet have different functions.

We cannot compare a fish to a bird and say the fish is worthless because it cannot fly, they were created for distinct purpose and environments! Sometimes we are guilty of trying to force our way into a space we weren't created for and come away feeling like there's something wrong with us..but just like when a plant stops growing, and we change the environment to help it to thrive..sometimes we need replanted. We cannot grow in toxicity, and sometimes it's not even necessarily a "bad" place but we outgrow it.. there are no gold stars or trophies given out for staying in a place forever when it lacks the things needed to help you continue to grow. Don't get me wrong, and think I'm telling you that when things get tough you have to leave..alot of times tough situations bring out the most growth in us..only God can tell you what is needed in your situation. I've been in both, where God told us to endure the hard things and also when He told us to go, neither of them are easy..but at different times both are necessary. Staying in the wrong place can cause or even amplify a spirit of rejection and the only spirit that should ever be encouraged in our lives is the Holy Spirit! In the right environment , with the right people,other spirits that may be present in our lives can be exposed in love and sent on their way..like pruning dead leaves or root rot..for the purpose of more growth and fruit!

Now, let's look at competition. As with lack, we may look at others and compare ourselves to them..but we aren't called to look like others, we are called to look like Jesus! So if He is the standard, we shouldn't be looking to others at all for approval, only to Him!

HEBREWS 12:1-2

THEREFORE, SINCE WE ARE SURROUNDED BY SUCH A HUGE CROWD OF WITNESSES TO THE LIFE OF FAITH, LET US STRIP OFF EVERY WEIGHT THAT SLOWS US DOWN, ESPECIALLY THE SIN THAT SO EASILY TRIPS US UP. AND LET US RUN WITH ENDURANCE THE RACE GOD HAS SET BEFORE US. 2 WE DO THIS BY KEEPING OUR EYES ON JESUS, THE CHAMPION WHO INITIATES AND PERFECTS OUR FAITH. BECAUSE OF THE JOY AWAITING HIM, HE ENDURED THE CROSS, DISREGARDING ITS SHAME. NOW HE IS SEATED IN THE PLACE OF HONOR BESIDE GOD'S THRONE.

I love the Message Version of this passage also:

DO YOU SEE WHAT THIS MEANS—ALL THESE PIONEERS WHO BLAZED THE WAY, ALL THESE VETERANS CHEERING US ON? **I**T MEANS WE'D BETTER GET ON WITH IT. **S**TRIP DOWN, START RUNNING—AND NEVER QUIT! **N**O EXTRA SPIRITUAL FAT, NO PARASITIC SINS. **K**EEP YOUR EYES ON **J**ESUS, WHO BOTH BEGAN AND FINISHED THIS RACE WE'RE IN. **S**TUDY HOW HE DID IT. **B**ECAUSE HE NEVER LOST SIGHT OF WHERE HE WAS HEADED—THAT EXHILARATING FINISH IN AND WITH GOD —HE COULD PUT UP WITH ANYTHING ALONG THE WAY: **C**ROSS, SHAME, WHATEVER. ∆ND NOW HE'S THERE, IN THE PLACE OF HONOR, RIGHT ALONGSIDE GOD. WHEN YOU FIND YOURSELVES FLAGGING IN YOUR FAITH, GO OVER THAT STORY AGAIN, ITEM BY ITEM, THAT LONG LITANY OF HOSTILITY HE PLOWED THROUGH. **T**HAT WILL SHOOT ADRENALINE INTO YOUR SOULS!

These verses show us that we cant afford to be looking at everyone else and how they do things..we have a specific race set before us! Imagine a race track where each lane had different obstacles, turns and challenges, and even different end results..if you were looking over at the person in the other lane instead of at your own track, you would trip and fall! In the Kingdom, we share the goal of spreading the gospel to the lost, but what works for some people doesn't work for others..God knows this and pursues each person in unique ways..and therefore we cannot all do the same thing. We are a part of the body of Christ..Jesus is the head and tells us each what to do. But a body cannot be completely made of the same parts, each has a specific job and function that serves the greater purpose..we must work together but still maintain our individual function.

For just as the body is one and has many members, and all the members of the body, though many, are one body, so it is with Christ. For in one Spirit we were all baptized into one body—Jews or Greeks, slaves or free—and all were made to drink of one Spirit. For the body does not consist of one member but of many. If the foot should say, "Because I am not a hand, I do not belong to the body," that would not make it any less a part of the body. And if the ear should say, "Because I am not an eye, I do not belong to the body," that would not make it any less a part of the body. If the whole body were an eye, where would be the sense of hearing? If the whole body were an ear, where would be the sense of smell? But as it is, God arranged the members in the body, each one of them, as he chose. If all were a single member, where would the body be? As it is, there are many parts, yet one body. The eye cannot say to the hand, "I have no need of you," nor again the head to the feet, "I have no need of you." On the contrary, the parts of the body that seem to be weaker are indispensable, and on those parts of the body that we think less honorable we bestow the greater honor, and our unpresentable parts are treated with greater modesty, which our more presentable parts do not require. But God has so composed the body, giving greater honor to the part that lacked it, that there may be no division in the body, but that the members may have the same care for one another. If one member suffers, all suffer together; if one member is honored, all rejoice together.

Now you are the body of Christ and individually members of it. And God has appointed in the church first apostles, second prophets, third teachers, then miracles, then gifts of healing, helping, administrating, and various kinds of tongues. Are all apostles? Are all prophets? Are all teachers? Do all work miracles? Do all possess gifts of healing? Do all speak with tongues? Do all interpret? But earnestly desire the higher gifts.
And I will show you a still more excellent way

1 Corinthians 12:12–31

This is why it is so vital for us not to compare ourselves with others..I know it's easier said than done, and we are all a work in progress..but I believe getting free from the spirit of competition, lack and comparison can help us so much to walk in our true identity. The God of the universe saw a need in the world, in His Kingdom- and made you specifically to fulfill the role! And sometimes we may be doing something similar to others, but you have a uniqueness about you..a different audience than others, you will reach people that they don't even know..so rather than thinking about yourself and why you don't need to do that because someone else already is..shift your focus onto the person/people that may be unreached if you do not obey what God told you to do on your path. Ask yourself, and ask God..is it worth it for just one person? The answer will always be yes! He leaves the 99 to go after the 1 every time, and if He is our example..we should too. Obedience matters far more than just for our own benefit..because God is so vastly and intricately weaving people together in His story that one thread out of place can have a ripple effect and cause the whole thing to be distorted. But God is also patient with us and often waits for our obedience..if you ignore His instruction, He will stop giving you more until you do the last thing He said. .because of His love, for us and the people we are called to reach. You can try and try to do other things to distract yourself, sometimes you may look at others and see their success and think "I could do that too..it's working for them" but when it doesn't, He'll be right there waiting for you to come back to the place you left Him, take your hand..and say, "let's go together"

So I want to leave you with a couple questions and give you time to ponder and pray on it. As with every question in this book, it is never for condemnation, shame or guilt..it is for observation and growth. Don't beat yourself up, just observe, repent when needed and ask God to help you start again..He's waiting

- WHAT WAS THE LAST THING GOD TOLD ME TO DO?

- HAVE I DONE IT YET?

- IF NOT, WHY?

- IF YES, WHAT HAPPENED?

- WHERE HAVE I ALLOWED LACK, COMPARISON AND COMPETITION TO STEAL MY JOY AND PURPOSE?

CHAPTER 6
THAT'S NOT MY NAME

Chapter 6
That's Not my Name

"That's not my name" Throughout the writing of this book, this phrase has repeated in my mind and I hear that song in my head from the Ting Tings. It's an upbeat and catchy song with a sad message about identity that I think speaks to how alot of us feel at times. We are given labels,and expectations that don't speak of who we are at all. Sometimes we try to force ourselves to be what others want, grasping for acceptance. On the outside we may be put together and look like we're all good, but behind the mask we're falling apart. I get it, we do what we have to do to survive. But if we want to walk in our true identity, we must release the versions of ourselves that we adopted/created to survive, so that we can thrive!

This entire book is meant to help you understand that it's ok to drop the mask for Jesus. We all long for someone to look at us in the crowd and see beyond the facade and really see us, and to care enough to talk. Jesus is that one. In His presence, you don't have to keep pretending. You can bare it all to Him, and you'll receive nothing but pure love from Him. Kingdom living isn't a constant state of fight or flight, it is not a people pleasing life. You may have heard that it is a life of dying to yourself, and the truth is-you've been doing that your whole life-living to please others, all the while you're slowly killing yourself ..trying to serve others and make sure you hold it all together for them, while you crack under the pressure..you're the fixer, but there's no time to tend to your wounds, there's always someone else who needs it more . But God never intended for you to carry that weight, and dropping it at His feet doesn't mean you've failed. It is the most beautiful act of surrender. When God asks us to "die to ourselves" He is doing that because the life He has for us is so much better! Yes, it can be painful at times to deny our flesh and desires, but I am a living testimony that every single time we do, He has given me better than I could've even imagined! His fire will fall on your sacrifice! All throughout scripture we hear of the miracles of Jesus and the people involved in them. What I've noticed Is that even still today we often refer to these people by their deficiency. Names like "blind bartimaeus", "doubting Thomas", "The woman with the issue of blood" etc. But God looked at these people beyond what others may have labeled them, beyond their name tags. Even with the woman at the well he knew that she was a samaritan woman and that Jews had no dealings with samaritans, But he didn't care about her label from the world he knew that his father truly loved her regardless of her ethnicity, regardless of her race ,her background of issues with rejection or with her reputation of being with many men. Jesus saw beyond the label in every one of these people's lives and he does the same today. It doesn't matter if you've been labeled a Black Sheep, weirdo ,wild child, prude, home wrecker, Socially awkward, addict-whatever it may be. In my life I've learned that people often label you something based off their perception of how you act or to make themselves feel better. They may accept someone else's story of you without actually getting to know you for themselves. When people don't understand someone or something they label it as a way of protecting themselves against it. But this is problematic. In scripture God tells us many times to get to know people, to create relationship with people, that's what Jesus himself did while he was on the Earth. He looked past every label of people.. it didn't matter if they were considered unclean, prostitutes, or drunks ,he sat with them. Not to be associated with them and not to accept their behavior. But to love them where they were and show them a better way. He is the same in our lives today, he comes to us in our darkest places.. maybe we are on the floor of a bathroom ready to swallow a handful of pills,maybe we are about to pull our hair out because we don't know how we can last one more day, maybe we are running from our lives,from the trauma that we've experienced by stuffing ourselves with food, drinks or relationships, or busyness looking for something to either fill the void,or distract us from it. And God will come and sit with us in the dark- not to join us and do what we're doing but to show us the way out. He will show you that there is another way. And when you surrender yourself to Him, He will save you, heal you, deliver you out of all of it! It probably won't happen all at once, because just like it took you years to get that deep, it will take time to heal. But what's so great about God is that He never gives up on us. Your story may be different than mine, and your process will look different too, because it's customized for you by your Creator. But I do know, if He's still giving you air to breathe and your heart is still beating, then there's still hope. There is still a purpose for you on this Earth that ONLY you can fulfill. And we cannot allow the opinions of others to dictate whether or not we fulfill it. They may not understand it, because they didn't create it..and that's ok. God has some secret missions for you and some people are on a need to know basis of that information..it's not their assignment, it's yours.

I want you to take some time and look back at the beginning pages of this book and reflect on the words you wrote about yourself, maybe some of these things are what others have said about you and you accepted them.

Now imagine that all of those words were tattooed all over your body. These are the things that people first see about you. Does that make you cringe or want to hide? We spend so much time these days trying to make ourselves appear better than we really are, hiding the reality that deep inside we are lost, and broken. But no amount of makeup, cute clothes, fancy cars, pintrest pretty houses or "perfection" will actually help to heal us. It is only in our honest vulnerability that we can finally begin to acknowledge the issues and begin to work on them and find healing.

So if you were covered with tattoos of all those ugly words, imagine that you come into the presence of God and show them to Him, with tear filled eyes and shaking hands you hand Him the shattered pieces of your heart and say "it's not much, but it's all I have" and He smiles at you and says "It's all I've ever wanted!" And as He lifts you up off the floor, those labels fall to the ground and disappear. He puts a robe of royalty over your shoulders and a crown on your head and says "daughter, you are mine" maybe your robe is purple, or maybe like Joseph's coat of many colors, or maybe its full of rhinestones that blind people when you walk, if I could chose mine it would probably have distressed denim and studs on it. But the point is, its unique to you..let people misunderstand you and call you names..but don't ever let them keep you from your purpose!

God's word is a love story to us, showing us time and time again how He pursues our hearts, even when we run away and settle for the lesser things of the world. Being firmly planted in His love will allow you to go through whatever part of the growth process is necessary. Whether you're in a season of hiding and your growth is happening underground or you're beginning to sprout or you're a well established, mighty oak tree..or if pruning is needed ..your foundation will be secure.

Your new identity awaits..I want you to begin to live from a place of knowing how deeply loved you are and seeking Him for the blueprints for your unique assignment on this Earth, not looking at what others are doing and copying them. And when others try to slap another label on you (and they will) if it doesn't align with what God says about you, I want you to say out loud "That's Not My Name!" And if you ever need a reminder, go to His word, get in His presence, ask Him and He will show you! Get in the habit of speaking His word over yourself..if you have to plaster your walls with sticky notes, do it..it's that important!

CHAPTER 7
Follow Me

Chapter 7
"Follow Me"

If I've learned anything on this journey, it is that even once God reveals to you who you are in Him, we can still sometimes get caught up in thinking "ok, now that I know who I am, what is my purpose or calling in life?" And we may start chasing after those things. I'm guilty of it too, so don't be too hard on yourself. But what I pray you have learned in this process up to this point is that everything you need, can only be found in Him! Don't allow your calling to become your idol. Don't let your pursuit of the vision God gave you of what you're supposed to do in this life take the place of pursuing the one who gave it to you in the first place. When you look at the disciples, think about when Jesus called them. (**John 1:35-51**) He just said "Follow Me" They left behind careers, family and things that had given them identity in the past, immediately when Jesus called Peter, he changed his name from Simon.. there was an identity shift from the get go. Names in the Bible often represented character traits, and God was making a statement here. We know that Peter wasn't immediately willing to lay his life down for Jesus, and he often put his foot in his mouth, he didn't understand why Jesus did certain things and questioned him.. but when his name was changed it was a prophetic moment where God said "on this rock, I will build my church" even before Peter was "solid" Jesus was looking at his future, and declaring it to everyone. When He calls us out of darkness, He gives us our new identity too, and it takes time to develop us and get us to see what He sees. But how do we get from where we are now to where He wants us to be? He simply says " Follow Me"
In our modern world we often want titles, positions etc that we can be proud of, and when it comes to our purpose we want to know all the things before they happen, we want blueprints and strategies, and that's all great, but when we don't get them as quickly as we'd like or they don't look how we thought, we often look to others to see how they're doing it, what's working for them, what do they have to say about it? Well that's where we get lost. Our calling is the same as the disciples.. to follow Jesus! And in that process of following, we are met with opportunities to help others, to pray for them, encourage them , to meet a need they have, to share the gospel, to heal the sick and set captives free! This is it.. in our everyday lives, at work, at the kids activities, at the grocery store, wherever you go. I have often seen how when we just abide in Him daily,simply because we love Him.. He will bring the right people, places and things to you.

Remember when David was a shepherd boy out in the field, his own father didn't think he was even worthy of being brought home to be considered for King..but God knew and told Samuel about him. (**1 Samuel 16**) And David went back to tending sheep right after..his reign did not begin for many years. He had many battles to fight in between and lots of maturing to do..but we know that he must have continued to spend time with God while tending sheep, because there is fruit of it in his life! It had become so ingrained in him that when he finally did get the crown, he didn't stop pursuing God, always asking Him what to do next. The Bible calls him "a man after God's own heart" . We know that David made mistakes at times and committed adultery and murder, but he didn't let even those things keep him from God..he chased after God continually. Whether he was in the fields with sheep, or on the throne, hiding in a cave from Saul or leading vast armies..he went to God. He led a life of repentance when he failed, because He couldn't imagine life without relationship with God.

My prayer is that we will be the same. That no matter where we are in life,in the valley or on the mountain top, whether we see our name in lights or feel unseen..that we would always go to God, not looking for what He can give us- but just because we love Him more. In His presence is where we find ourselves. You can be sure that God will test you at times. It's easy to say we love Him, but do our actions show it? If you were in a relationship with someone who always told you they loved you, but never had time for you or even when they sat next to you they felt a million miles away..you would begin to have trust issues..you wouldn't believe their words anymore. Maybe from the outside people think your relationship is good, but it's all just for show. Sometimes we're the same way with God. We go to church and go through the motions of what we think it's supposed to look like, we know all the scriptures and lyrics..we may even give other people advice..but if we're really honest, things are not ok. Maybe your life has gotten hectic and heavy, and you don't feel like worshiping God, maybe you're full of guilt and shame and don't feel worthy of going to Him,the truth is..even at your best you're still not worthy..its only by His blood that we can be made right with him. God doesn't want your lip service and pretend worship..it means no more to Him than it does to you. He wants your heart- raw, messy, and real. Because only when we are vulnerable and honest with the things we feel and are carrying can we begin to truly worship Him. Stop trying to hold all the pieces of your broken heart together with tattered thread to make yourself "presentable" to God..He sees the mess, it doesn't scare Him. He's not intimidated by your fear, anger, worry,or sadness. Usually it's us who don't want to face the truth of our situation, but it is prideful to be falling apart and unwilling to accept help.

When we lay our burdens down, it often will lead us into worship. If you go through and read the Psalms of David, they often start out expressing his fears, his enemies surrounding him, his depression etc..but as it progresses he begins to change his worry into worship. A divine exchange is made in the secret place, where what at first seems too big for us to carry or endure, becomes so small in comparison to God. And He changes our perspective. This is a privilege and part of our inheritance as children of the Most High. When we are overwhelmed, we can crawl up on Daddy's lap and just fall apart, but as we do, He will put us back together. We can come out of our time with Him full of joy and peace, even if the circumstances haven't changed. Stay in this place. I've spent my fair share of days, weeks and months just trying to hold it all together. Feeling the weight of the world dragging my broken heart on the floor. Constantly choking back tears, sometimes venting just enough to relieve the pressure, but never getting full release. The world is heavy, life is heavy. And I'm often baffled at just how much emotion and spiritual weight are held behind our seemingly thin human flesh. It's as if our human body acts as a dam to hold back the oceans we hold inside. But I've learned over time that we were never meant to hold it, we're meant to flow..the dam will break at some point. The enemy loves to pile on the list of things you need, and demands, with a side of guilt and shame if you can't measure up, and another helping of inadequacy if you have to ask for help or say no to something. He is all too ready to use the trauma from your past against you too. He will continue dumping more and more on you until you're drowning. But God will use that breaking point to show you that He is always there. Just like the seed comes undone to bring forth growth and new life, I declare every broken place inside of you is just the start of what God has planned for you.

This journey of looking for our identity has led us to the One who gave it to us, because they are intertwined and inseparable. If it's true that we look most like the 5 people we are closest to in life, may we never leave His presence. May our existence in the world be a reflection of Him and the time we spend with Him. Like the sun shining on a disco ball, let His glory shine on us as we reflect Him to those around us. May what He calls us ring louder than any other name we are given. May we rise to our true selves and our name be Imago Dei "Image Bearer"

HELLO MY NAME IS	HELLO MY NAME IS
FREE — John 8:36	**HEALED** — Isaiah 53:5
SAFE — Psalm 91	**NEW** — 2 Corinthians 5:17
DAUGHTER — 1 John 3:2	**VICTORIOUS** — Romans 8:37
MASTERPIECE — Ephesians 2:10	**WHOLE** — Colossians 2:10

HELLO MY NAME IS CHOSEN
EPHESIANS 1:4

HELLO MY NAME IS LOVED
JOHN 3:16

HELLO MY NAME IS SEEN
GENESIS 16:13

HELLO MY NAME IS KNOWN
JEREMIAH 1:5

HELLO MY NAME IS BEAUTIFUL
PSALM 139:13-14

HELLO MY NAME IS BLESSED
EPHESIANS 1:3

HELLO MY NAME IS CALLED
ROMANS 8:29

HELLO MY NAME IS FORGIVEN
EPHESIANS 1:7

Made in the USA
Columbia, SC
07 February 2025